LEARN TO DRAW

YOUR FAVORITE
Disney · PIXAR
CHARACTERS

Get ready to draw the best of the best
from the blockbuster Disney/Pixar films!
From **Woody** and **Buzz** to **Sulley** and **Mike**
to **Nemo** and **Marlin,** this book is full of all
your favorite animated characters. And inside
you'll find out how to draw them all, just like
the pros. So grab some paper and sharpen
your skills (and your pencil)—
then turn the page
to get started!

Choosing Tools and Materials

In this book, you'll meet a lot of fun characters to draw! All you need is a pencil and an eraser to start, but you'll also to want to color the whole cast so they really stand out. Try colored markers, colored pencils, crayons, or even watercolor or acrylic paints. Let your imagination run wild, and make your favorite characters as bright and colorful as you like!

drawing pencil and paper

eraser

sharpener

felt-tip markers

paintbrush and paints

colored pencils

Getting Started

Let's start with the basics. Just follow these simple steps, and you'll be amazed at how fun and easy drawing can be!

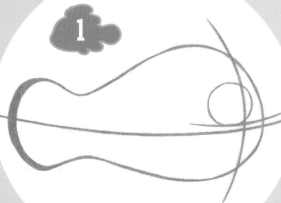

Step 1
First draw the basic shape of the character. Then add some simple guidelines to help you place the features.

Step 2
Each new step is shown in blue.

Step 3
Simply follow the blue lines to add the details.

Step 4
Now darken the lines you want to keep and erase the rest.

Step 5
Use crayons, markers, colored pencils, or paints to add vivid colors.

Flik

Flik is a lovable worker ant whose inventions are often brilliant but disastrous. Clumsy and easily excited, Flik is known for his uncanny ability to make things go wrong. But his ideas are what ultimately save the ant colony from Hopper and his gang.

The 2 parts of Flik's antennae form a right angle.

NO!

YES!

The first antenna segments are like tapered straws.

With antennae, he's about 5 heads tall.

step 1

step 2

Flik has 3 toes.

Flik's torso is like a bowling pin.

His abdomen is like a bowling ball.

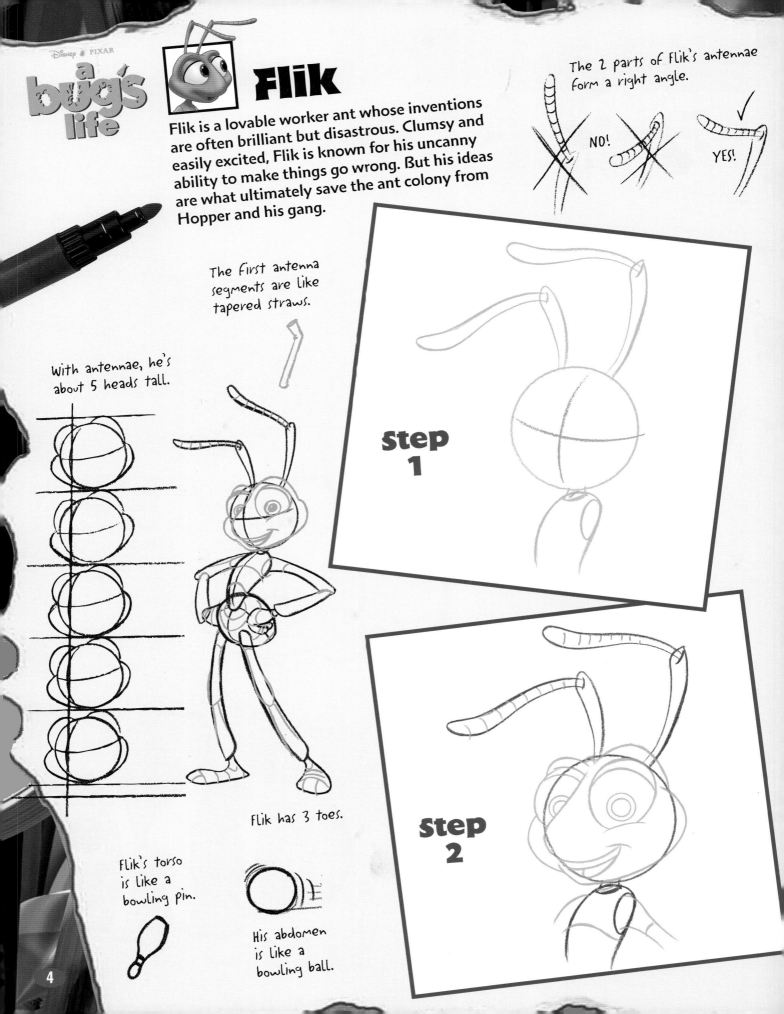

Expressions

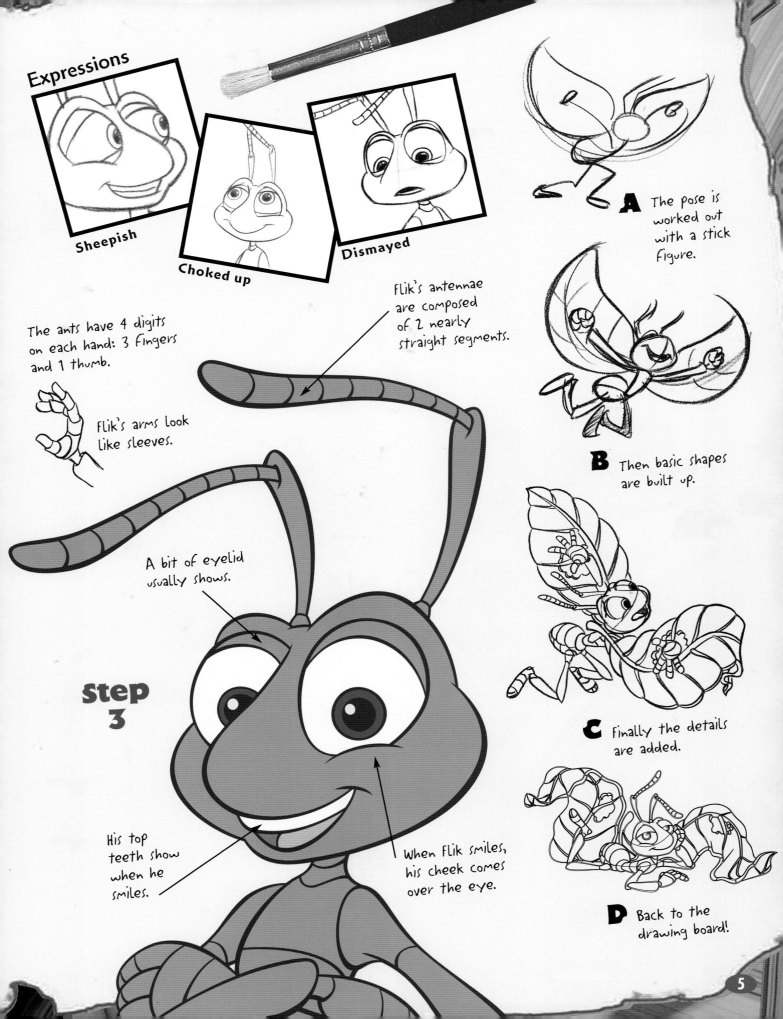

Sheepish

Choked up

Dismayed

The ants have 4 digits on each hand: 3 fingers and 1 thumb.

Flik's arms look like sleeves.

Flik's antennae are composed of 2 nearly straight segments.

A The pose is worked out with a stick figure.

B Then basic shapes are built up.

C Finally the details are added.

D Back to the drawing board!

A bit of eyelid usually shows.

Step 3

His top teeth show when he smiles.

When Flik smiles, his cheek comes over the eye.

Atta

Atta is the stressed-out princess who is in training to become leader of the ant colony. She has the makings of a good queen, but she's still learning. Flik often flusters her with his unconventionality, but there is something in the back of Atta's mind that tells her that Flik and his ideas are worthy of consideration.

Atta's eyes are elliptical.

The tiara is made of leaves.

Atta's tiara has a jewel: a tiny drop of amber.

step 1

She always has 3 long eyelashes.

The nose is pointy in profile.

Step 2

Surprised

Annoyed

Concerned

Each eyelid covers 1/3 of the eye.

Wings and curled antennae are characteristics of royalty.

The veins emerge from the base of the wing.

Atta is about 4-1/2 heads tall.

Atta has a football-shaped head in 3/4 view.

✓ YES

✗ NO

Atta's nose is just suggested.

Step 3

Her fingers are much more tapered than Flik's.

Her arms and legs are shapely.

Her feet are also more tapered than Flik's.

Dot

Princess Dot is the adorable daughter of the Queen and little sister to Princess Atta. She is innocent and wide-eyed, but she is also spunky and tomboyish. Dot is the only one who believes in Flik in times of trouble.

This is Princess Dot's Blueberry uniform. The cape is a leaf.

step 1

step 2

Dot is shaped a lot like you-know-who.

Her eyes sit on the midline of the face.

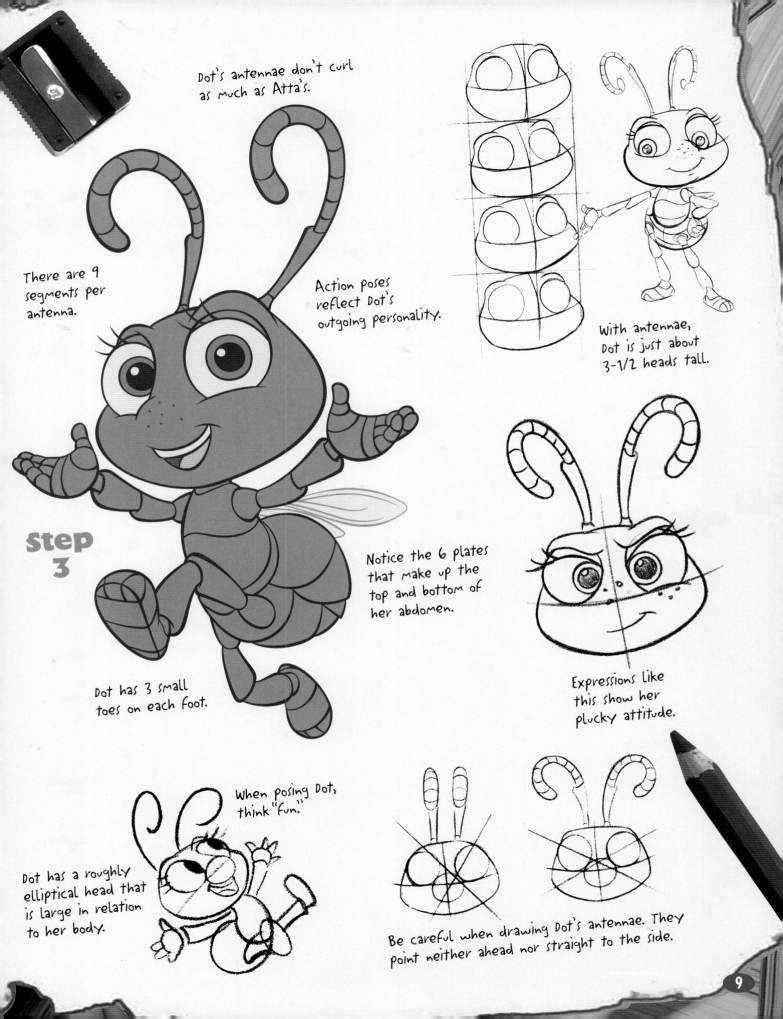

Dot's antennae don't curl as much as Atta's.

There are 9 segments per antenna.

Action poses reflect Dot's outgoing personality.

With antennae, Dot is just about 3-1/2 heads tall.

Step 3

Notice the 6 plates that make up the top and bottom of her abdomen.

Dot has 3 small toes on each foot.

Expressions like this show her plucky attitude.

When posing Dot, think "fun."

Dot has a roughly elliptical head that is large in relation to her body.

Be careful when drawing Dot's antennae. They point neither ahead nor straight to the side.

Buzz Lightyear

Buzz has stars in his eyes until Woody pulls him back down to earth. For most of **Toy Story,** Buzz doesn't understand that he's a toy. But in **Toy Story 2,** he understands so well that he has to remind Woody.

Buzz's chin takes up about 1/3 of his head

keep brows thick

iris is about 1/3 eye size

YES!   NO!

brow should barely touch eye in normal pose or else he looks mad

STEP 1

STEP 2

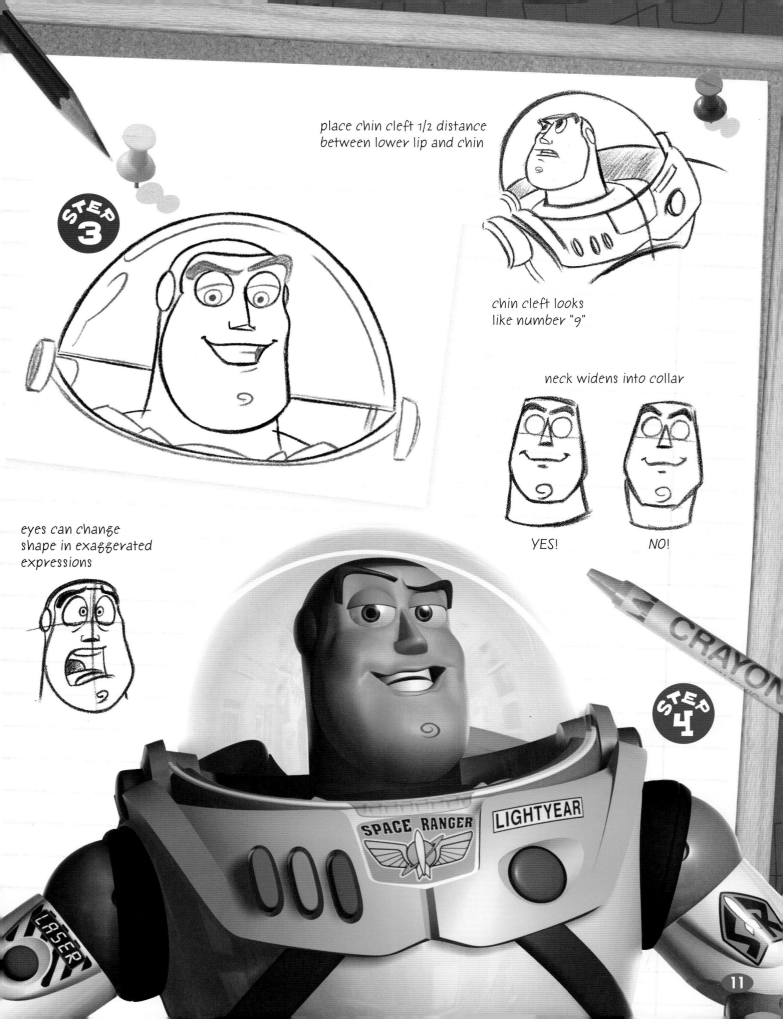

place chin cleft 1/2 distance between lower lip and chin

STEP 3

chin cleft looks like number "9"

neck widens into collar

YES!   NO!

eyes can change shape in exaggerated expressions

SPACE RANGER   LIGHTYEAR

STEP 4

CRAYON

LASER

11

WOODY

Woody is top toy in both **Toy Story** and **Toy Story 2**. That's a tough spot to share, especially with a new toy, named Buzz Lightyear, who thinks he's a space ranger. But Woody takes it all in stride. After all, he's one tough cowboy. And he's smart enough to know that the best part about being a toy is having a special kid like Andy to play with.

STEP 1

STEP 2

ears are flat on top

hair curl
is like the
letter "C"

round eyes

large iris
(1/2 of eye)

bottom half of head
shows off Woody's
handsome square
jawline

STEP 3

STEP 4

too
straight

NO!   NO!   YES!   show nostril
side on 3/4
view or
profile

teeth are **1**
long rectangle

YES!   NO!

Jessie

Jessie knows what it means to be a toy. She once belonged to a little girl who loved her as much as Andy loves Woody. But that little girl gave her away, and the brokenhearted toy decided that being a collectible is better than being with a child who might outgrow you. Woody has to remind Jessie what being a toy is all about—and convince her to come back to Andy's room with him.

STEP 1

5 pieces of fringe attach to outside edge of chaps

chaps wrap around front of jeans

chaps looser on bottom to allow for boots

stitching wraps around cuff

shirt and gauntlet pattern

3 fringe pieces

YES!

NO!

she has a button nose

her hat usually sits on the back of her head

Woody's hat is triangular

Jessie's hat is rounder

pull-string on back

torso is shaped like a peanut

STEP 2

STEP 3

STEP 4

keep rag-doll body flexible

Sulley

"RRROAR!" Although Sulley scares kids for a living, he really has a heart of gold and is an all-around nice guy. Sulley's a gentle giant who would never hurt anyone—especially not a kid! When he discovers that scaring them might not be the best thing for kids, he decides to do something about it, which changes Monsters, Inc., forever.

STEP 1

STEP 2

eyelid is rounded like this **YES!** **NO!**

YES! eyebrows overlap like this . . .

. . . and this

NO! not separated like this

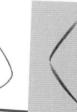

outside of horn has angles; inside is curved

YES! bend knees to show weight

NO! don't make legs too straight

STEP 3

STEP 4

STEP 5

draw big hands with pointed nails

don't round out toes

YES!

NO!

Mike

Both best friend and scare assistant to James P. Sullivan, Mike Wazowski is proud of his job, and he loves the perks that go along with it. Mike wouldn't change a thing about his life—except maybe to eliminate all the paperwork he has to do. A little green ball of energy, Mike is always ready with a joke and a smile, especially for his best girl, Celia.

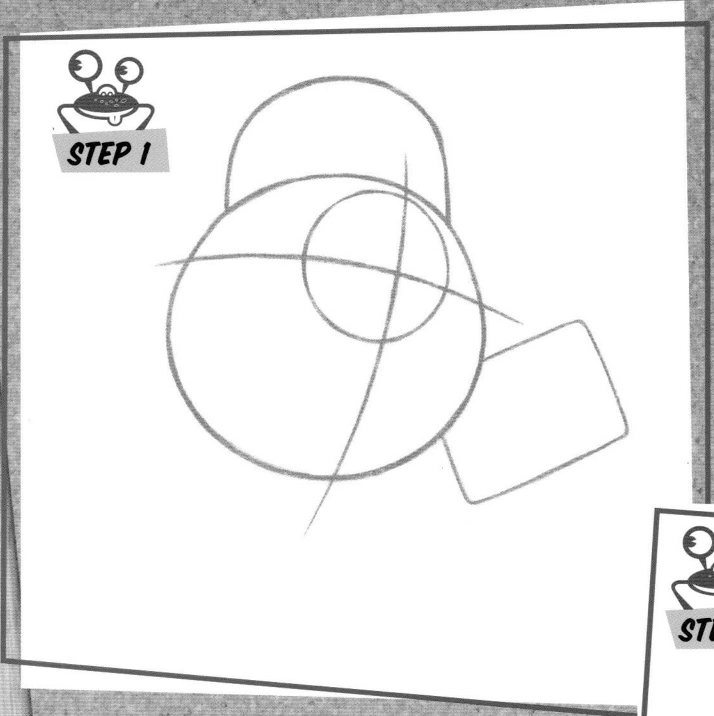

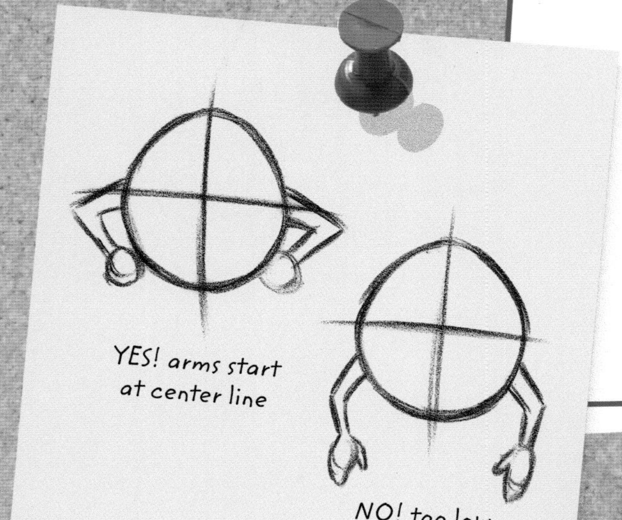

STEP 1

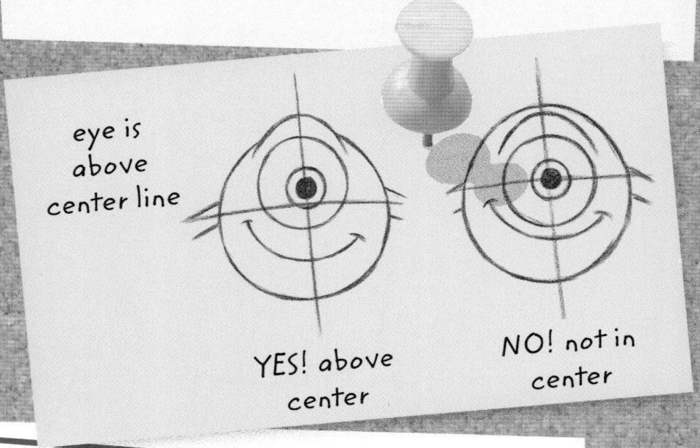

STEP 2

eye is above center line

YES! above center

NO! not in center

YES! arms start at center line

NO! too low

FOR YOUR SAFETY:

DO NOT FEED THE DISPATCHER

Boo

Don't be scared—Boo is just the name that Sulley gave to the little girl who journeyed through her closet door into Monstropolis. Adorable and extremely curious, Boo isn't afraid of Mike and Sulley—but they're plenty afraid of her! Completely unaware that she might be in danger, Boo is in no rush to go back to the human world; she's having too much fun in Monstropolis!

Powerful Screamer

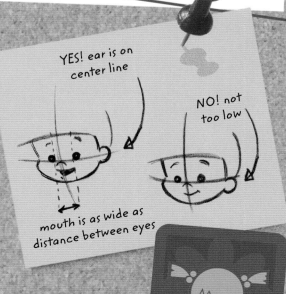

STEP 1

YES! hands are small with short, round fingers

NO! not long and squared

YES! ear is on center line

NO! not too low

mouth is as wide as distance between eyes

STEP 2

STEP 3

YES! pigtails are rounded like this

NO! not straight like this

STEP 4

STEP 5

YES! big breaks in hair

NO! not little triangles

Boo

Nemo
Clownfish

Here's Nemo—the adventurous little fish with the "lucky" fin who longs for excitement and friends to play with. But instead, he's saddled with an overprotective single dad who never lets the poor little guy out of his sight.

Well, one day, Nemo dares to show his friends he's not scared of the ocean (the way his dad is), and he swims off alone. He ends up getting a lot more excitement than he bargained for! But he also discovers just how brave and resourceful he can be.

from side, Nemo is shaped like a Goldfish® cracker

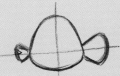

from front, body looks like a gumdrop

"lucky" fin is wedge-shaped with notch cut out

YES! rays follow curve of fin

NO! too straight and even

YES! varied stripe shapes

NO! too similar and too straight

YES! top (dorsal) fin is 2 different shapes pointing at different angles

NO! too even; too upright

4

top fin is same height as 1 eye

3

Nemo is about 4 "eyes tall" including top fin

4
3
2
1
0

YES! bottom fins are set apart from each other

NO! fins look like bow tie

5

Marlin

Clownfish

Marlin is Nemo's dad—the not-so-funny clownfish. After losing almost all his family, he became a little crazy about doing everything possible to keep his only son safe from the dangerous ocean. Unfortunately he goes a little overboard and won't allow Nemo to do anything—he doesn't even let Nemo go to school!

He fusses and frets a lot, but he really does mean well. It takes a little journey across the ocean, and meeting up with Dory, to teach him the meaning of trust and letting go. When it comes down to it, he's just a regular dad who will do anything for his son.

Marlin is about 2 times the size of Nemo

rays on Marlin's fins
and tail radiate out
from "meaty" parts of
body like this . . .

"meaty" parts

. . . not like this

face is kind
of flat

5 rays on side
(pectoral) fins
and tail

from side, shaped
like turkey
drumstick

bags under
eyes make
him look tired

YES!
eyes close
together

NO! eyes
too far apart

Dory

Regal Blue Tang

Dory is one chatty, friendly, funny fish! She never gives up hope—when things get tough, she just keeps on swimming. Always willing and helpful, Dory has everything going for her except for one small thing—her memory. She can't remember anything! But she risks her own life to help Marlin find Nemo (despite the fact that she can't remember the little guy's name!).

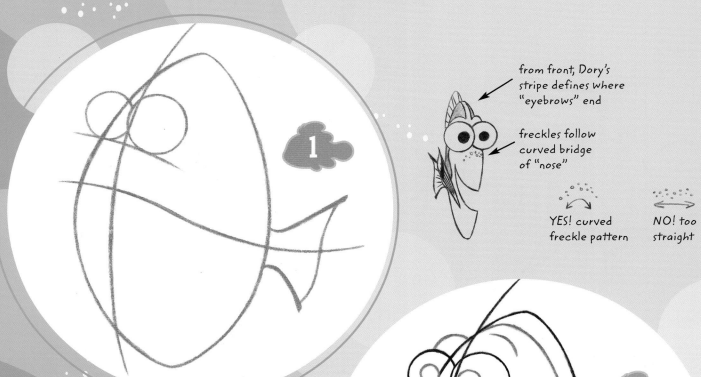

from front, Dory's stripe defines where "eyebrows" end

freckles follow curved bridge of "nose"

YES! curved freckle pattern

NO! too straight

Dory is just over 4 times the size of Nemo

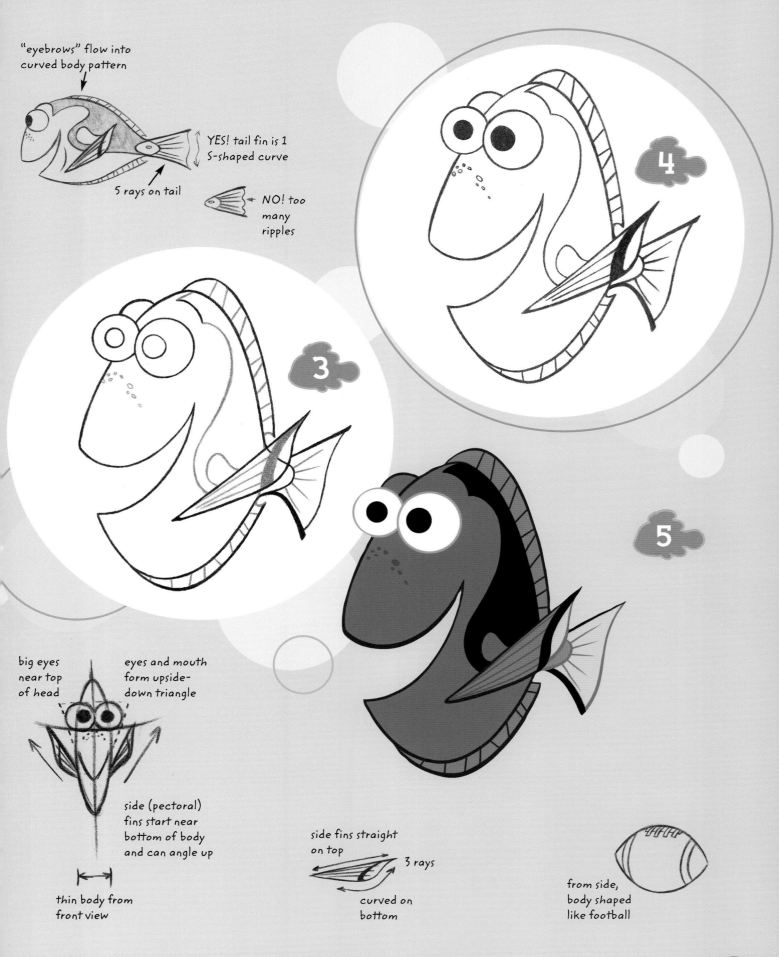

"eyebrows" flow into curved body pattern

YES! tail fin is 1 S-shaped curve

5 rays on tail

NO! too many ripples

3

4

5

big eyes near top of head

eyes and mouth form upside-down triangle

side (pectoral) fins start near bottom of body and can angle up

thin body from front view

side fins straight on top

3 rays

curved on bottom

from side, body shaped like football

MR. INCREDIBLE

A man of super strength, Mr. Incredible was once the best-known, most popular Super alive! Then, through the Super Relocation Program, Mr. Incredible became "normal" Bob Parr, a claims adjuster at probably the worst insurance company ever. But Bob is not content with his ordinary life. He misses being a Super. One day, a mysterious summons calls the hero back to action. . . .

STEP 1

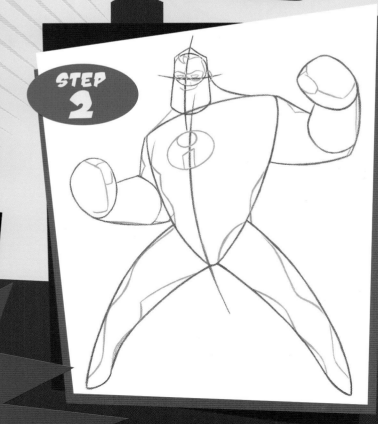

STEP 2

ELASTIGIRL

No one is as flexible as Elastigirl, a Super with an incredible reach! She could stretch her arm and land a punch before the crooks knew what hit them! But, as Helen Parr, Bob's wife and a mother of three, her Super powers are kept secret and largely unused—that is, until she finds out her Super spouse needs help! "Leave the saving of the world to the men? I don't think so!"

STEP
1

body shape is almost like a figure 8

STEP
2

STEP **3**

keep
bridge of
nose short

YES!
short

NO!
not long

STEP **4**

STEP **5**

Helen's hair is
not completely
round—there
is a series of
flattened areas

FLAT

FLAT

FLAT

FROZONE

Frozone was once known as the coolest Super on the planet. With the ability to create ice from the moisture in the air, he could build ice bridges, skate across them with special boots, and freeze criminals right in their tracks. Known as Lucius Best in his secret life, Frozone is also Mr. Incredible's best friend—and a reluctant partner in Bob's undercover heroics.

STEP 1

STEP 2